The Real Purpose of Networking

Milton Kelly

The Real Purpose Of Networking

Milton Kelly

Copyright © 2013 Milton Kelly

ISBN-10: 1482362007 **(CreateSpace)**
ISBN-13: 978-1482362008 **(CreateSpace)**
ASIN: B00BP1V4NK **(Amazon Kindle)**
ISBN: 9781304074164 **(Lulu)**

DEDICATION

This book is in dedication to the following individuals or groups: BDPA-NY Chapter of BDPA National, Reginald Christian and Black Creatives: The Premier Network for Multicultural Talent Group, Darryl Cherry and DC Real Talk Group, Georgia Woodbine and GW Network, Ovit Pursley and Recycling Black Dollars Group, Donna Jarrett and It Takes A Village Today Group, Anointed 4 Fellowship Networking Group and Create Your Own Opportunity Networking Group. Michelle Davis and The Metro Works Employment Ministries of Metropolitan Baptist Church of Newark, NJ.

CONTENTS

INTRODUCTION

The purposes for me to write this book are for the following reasons. A lot of individuals don't know what networking is all about. Some don't believe in networking. Some have the wrong idea about what networking is all about. There are a lot of common mistakes when individuals are networking. They don't know what their real purpose of networking. Some think that if they just attend a networking event, then they think that they are networking. They are so wrong. Some don't know how to behave when they are networking. In this book **"The Real Purpose of Networking"** I will show exactly the importance of networking. What is networking really all about? What to do and not to do when you are networking. To show different ways how you can network. This book is perfect for individuals such as Business Owners, Professionals, Students and people who are looking for a job. I will show you how you can have a successful networking experience. There is more about networking than going to a networking event. Networking really starts after the networking events when you start your follow up. A lot of people don't realize the importance of the follow up. The lack of the follow up is the main reason why a lot of individuals don't have a successful networking experience.

A lot of people are very clueless about networking. Some think that just because they are attending an event that they are networking. Some will go to an event to start with selling products at a networking event. There are some that after the event they will not do their follow up. The follow up is the beginning process of building relationship in which is the most important factor of networking. Some don't realize that when you are networking that you have to be communicated with others. Also a lot of individuals don't know the purpose of being part of a networking group. In this book I will tell you about the benefits of being a member of a networking group. I will also tell you about how to behave while you are networking.

In this book **"The Real Purpose of Networking"** I will also show the different ways on how you can do you follow up with your potential

Connections. I will tell you the function of networking groups and the purpose of becoming a member of a networking group. This book will help you to have a better understanding about networking. You will understand on how to build a solid relationship by networking. You will learn about how to mingle with others. Networking wasn't easy for me either but I learned as I kept on going to different events to network. We talk to people every day and doesn't realize that we have the opportunity to networking with people that we already know. Networking is another way of introducing yourself to others and getting to know each other better. Without networking you will not get too far. There are different steps on how you can have an awesome networking experience. The key of having an awesome networking experience is being social with others. Communications is the key to network and without it you will not be able to network with each other's. Everybody has their own way of networking. In this book I am going to show you in my way on how my networking experiences was successful for me.

CHAPTER 1

THE PURPOSE OF NETWORKING

"Networking is a common synonym for developing and maintain contacts and personal connections with a variety of people who might be helpful to you, your career or your business."

The question that you are asking me right now **"What is networking?" Or "What is the purpose of networking?** Networking is a common synonym for developing and maintains contacts and personal connections with a variety of people who might be helpful to you, your career or your business. Networking is a social experience where you connect and meet new people. In today's world that networking is very important in the job market and in the business world. Have you ever heard the saying, "It's not what you know, it's **WHO** you know?" While good business or opportunity isn't exactly a popularity contest, but networking is the important key. When I had lost my job in late 2007 I was in the process of looking for another job. I was looking in the classified ads in the newspaper but there weren't that much job posted. That's when I realized that most jobs are posted online. Employers are no longer giving out applications to you in person. Now you have to fill out an application online to apply for a job. At that time I had never heard about networking until after I went to an outplacement company. I had even gone to several employment agencies to apply for temporary jobs. They mentioned to me that I need to post my resume online at their website. They also mentioned that they have jobs for me and I told them that I was very interested in applying for them. After I shown them my interest in the job, I didn't hear from them since. So I had decided to give them a call myself to see the status of the job. They even lied to me that the job was still available or they did not return my call. Later on in the journey of my job search, I realized that those jobs websites were all clogged up with resumes from job seekers. The employers will not respond back to you until 8 months later or never call you. Several people had told me that I need to start to network. At that time I still didn't know anything about networking. I didn't start to learn how to network when I started to working with Primerica as an Independent Representative. All of the training that I had learned from our weekly training at Primerica. That's how I had really learned about how to network with my prospect clients. We had done a lot of building relationship with our clients. **Networking is all about** *who likes you and who respects you.* There is a difference between knowing someone or having someone know you and having someone like you and respect you. Before working with you or referring you to someone else, a successful person is conscious or subconsciously asking himself, *"Do I like and respect this person enough to put my reputation on the line by working with her or by introducing her to someone I trust?* If their answer is **"no,"** networking will get you nowhere. However, if the answer is **"yes,"** then you will encounter so much open door of new opportunities.

That's one of the reasons why networking is very important for job seekers. With networking you will have the opportunity to meet individuals from different backgrounds and companies. You will also meet business owners as well. People also can refer you to their friends, family members, their clients and their networks. They can also refer you to their contacts at different companies that you have an interest to work at. Usually people who network on a regular basis will have a better chance for career opportunities than people who are looking for jobs the traditional ways. Speaking of that the old traditional ways of looking for a job is not happening today. A lot of employers are not posting their job openings in the classified ads. Networking is the key to getting jobs in today's job market. People are getting jobs through individuals that they have relationships with. Networking is not Favoritism at all. You need to add value to other people and organizations or networking will get you nowhere. There is nothing unethical about engaging in networking to advance your career. Your network is your new position

Networking Consists of the following important key components:

- **People, Connect, Socials, Relationships, Contacts, Common, Planning, Efficiency, Interests, Support, Meeting, Mutual, Informal, Success, Strategies, Interaction, Business, Opportunities, Community, Jobs, Professionals, Branding, Online, Groups and Marketing**

These are the key components that will make up a successful networking experience. The Networking experience can be a great opportunity for meeting new people or friends. This experience is great for connections, searching for new opportunities such as jobs and business deals. Networking is usually in a professional environment. When you are networking you should always be professional. Networking is not going to be easy, but it takes a lot of hard work on your part. It is not a one day or an overnight experience, but a long process. Communications is the most important component of networking. Without communication you will not have a successful networking experience. I will explain more about networking further in this book. You need to be patience. You should be able to communicate or mingle with others. If you are not a people person then networking will not work out for you at all.

.

Networking is also great for professionals and business owners as well. With networking it will give you a chance to meet new people and new opportunities. Business owners are always looking forward to expand their business or finding new opportunities. Professionals always looking for ways to connect with other professionals, especially within their industries. Also they are willing to look for new connections and new opportunities. Networking is also great for partnership, such as events, projects and etc. When you are networking you should not be asking for a job or pushing to sell your products and services. Again networking is a process. First you need to make an introduction so you can get acquainted with each other especially if you don't know that person. Your purpose of networking is to get to know that person and working on to start to build a relationship. This is a great chance for you to make an introduction and give a minute pitch of what you do. They will do the exact same thing with you. Communication is the main key component for networking.

Marketing or making a brand of you is another important component of networking. We have to learn how to market ourselves. We can't hide behind a company or our business cards because we are actually the brand. We have to sell ourselves to others. What kind of images that you are representing. Again, you can't have a negative mindset. You need to have a positive mindset and have confidence in yourself. People will notice if you have lack of confidence or you have a negative mindset. When you are attending a networking event make sure you are mingle with others. You should never be late for a networking event. You should arrive at least 15 minutes before the event starts that way you can get a chance to have more time to mingle with others. Also you will have a chance to meet and talk with the organizer of the event. You don't want to be late because you really don't want to miss anything at the event. Also, you don't want to disturb anyone who is attending the event. These events are very informal. You will get a lot of information and tools to help you with being successful in your business and career. This is just like going to a seminar. You should always have plenty of business cards with you.

Let me ask you a question, **"What is your real purpose for networking?"** I attended so many networking events and I noticed that most people really don't have a clue what networking is really about. They don't make an effort to have a clear plan for their networking efforts. They don't even take the time to acquire a clearer understanding about how to effectively network to grow their business or career opportunities. They hope by attending events or meetings that they are going to be introduced to others. They also think by attending networking events that they are going to get opportunities overnight, but it does not happen at all. Again it is all a long process that you must follow. Look at the word **"Network"** you will notice that you don't see net-**SIT** or net-**AUTOMATIC** in the word **"NETWORK,"** but you will see **WORK** in the word **"NETWORK."** You will have to put some work into your networking. You can't afford to be lazy when you are networking. When you don't put the work in then you are going to miss out on your blessings and opportunities. Also in the word **"NETWORK," you** will never see net-**OVERNIGHT** in the word **"NETWORK."** Networking is work, but it is not hard at all if you have the right purpose and plan of actions. Networking is not favoritism at all. You need to add value to other people and organizations or your experience of networking will get you nowhere. There is nothing unethical about engaging in networking to advance your career. Here's the truth about networking. **Networking is all about** *who will likes you* *and who will respect you.* There is a difference between knowing someone and having someone that's known you and having someone like you and respect you. Before that person is willing to work with you or referring you to someone else that person who is successful will consciously or subconsciously asking this question for themselves **"Do I like that person enough to respect or trust?"** If their answer is **"no,"** networking will get you nowhere. However, if the answer is **"yes,"** then you as a professional can usually get almost anyone to open the door to that new opportunity. It is very important that you come prepared like what you are going plan to say and know what your purpose of networking are when you are attending an event. You need to scope out your surroundings that you are comfortable with. You also need to plan your time in advance. The point of networking is to participate and not to sit back and watch while others are working their network to develop connections.

You need to find your purpose for networking and attending networking events. There are so many reasons for attending networking events. Regardless of what your reasons or purpose is that you need to have an understanding that it is not about getting sales at the networking events. The purpose of attending networking events is the process of building relationships. Remember people will only do business or give opportunities to those individuals that they know and trust. The purpose of networking is to understand the power of people. Networking is about concentrating on the focus on bringing together successful, motivated professionals to help each other to become even more successful by meeting new people to create connections that will take their careers or business to the next level and beyond. The purpose of networking should be about growth. If you are not looking to achieve growth then you are wasting your time of networking. The purpose for networking should be about community for business like minded individuals. It should be about support from both ends. Support should go both ways. Networking with professional individuals is working as a team. There is no **"I"** in the word **"team."** Another word you should all be working together. There should be unity or harmony when you are networking. The purpose of networking should not be about hanging out business cards trying to hustle people for business. Networking is generally a community of **support, concern,** **upliftment,** and **empowerment.** Networking should consist of the following components such as **Professionalism, Consistency, Reliability, Intelligence, Resourcefulness, Strength, and Forward Thinking.** Here is the breakdown of the following Components of networking:

- **Professionalism**- Conducting oneself with responsibility, integrity, accountability and excellence. It means communicating effectively and appropriately and always finding a way to be productive.

- **Consistency**- Harmony of conduct or practice with profession.

- **Reliability**- The quality or state of being reliable.

- **Intelligence**- The act of understanding or applying knowledge.

- **Resourcefulness**- Able to meet situations and capable of devising ways and means.

- **Strength**- The quality or state of being strong: capacity for exertion or endurance.

- **Forward Thinking**- A person or company who is seen as visionary. Someone who is forward thinking is thinking progressively and possesses the ability to look beyond the **"NOW"** and formulates strategies for future success.

These are the key components that you need to possess to achieve an awesome networking experience. Networking is about building relationships with people you meet. You will want to go with the plan to have the knowledge that it is the part of your networking and marketing experience but not the only part. The best part of having great networking experiences is the follow up. I will explain more about follow up further in this book.

Milton Kelly

CHAPTER 2

THE NETWORKING EVENT

"Alone We Can Do So Little; Together We Can Do So Much."~~Helen Keller

One way that you can network is by attending networking events. There is always networking events that are being planned daily. Networking events usually consist of a meeting or social gatherings with a group of individuals such as professionals, entrepreneurs and etc. The networking events are a great way of connecting or meeting new people. Networking events are usually created by either an organizer or a professional group. This event can be a breakfast meeting, lunch meeting, evening meeting such as happy hour social gathering and dinner. These networking events can be free or a ticket event. Networking event usually has a meet and greet reception either at a bar or a restaurant. Most of the times you are required to purchase food and drink. Networking events could also be at a company office as well. Usually the food and drinks at the office are free but you may still have to pay a small fee to help with the costs of having the event there. Regardless if it is free or not, the events are still a great way to connect with others. At the networking events there are usually having an information session as well with a guest speaker to help with you with your business or career. You should definitely take full advantage of opportunities that you will encounter. Opportunities will not come knocking on your door; you will have to go out there to receive it. That's why it is very important to make an effort to go to networking events.

When you are attending a networking event you should try to take some notes while the guest speaker is speaking to the crowd about a particular topic. You do get a lot of great knowledge and wisdom from the guest speaker at these events. They are experts of what they are talking about because of their expertise and experiences. They want to share their knowledge with you. As I am writing this book I had attended so many networking events about every week and sometimes twice a day. I had met a lot of people at these events. Some of them had ended up being great connections for me and that's why I am writing my book today. There are always great connections that you can connect with but you will have to put the work in your networking. You may also meet someone by chance that will help you to find out what your passions or talents that you didn't realize that you have possess. Everybody has a passion in something. Like an individual that had an experience of being unemployed and think that their life is over, but you will eventually meet that special person that might have an opportunity just for you with your name on it. They may also lead you to the right person that you need to connect with as well. By me attending so many networking events I met up with some connections that were just right for me. So many times that how I found out that my gift is to help people and give back to the community. That is what my passion is all about. That's the main reason that I am following my passion of helping people is by writing my books and tell my story on how I had overcome my issues. This is actually my third book that I am writing right now. My first two books **"Walking In God's Path Toward Your Destination Volume 1" Change Your Mindset** and **"Walking In God's Path Toward Your Destination Volume 2" Building A Personal Relationship With Him.** Both of these books are Inspirational and motivational books that will help anyone to be empower, encourage, and uplifted, to have self esteem and faith. You may also meet someone that might help steer you to start your own small business or nonprofit. That person can lead you to the right connection either an individual or an organization. Again if you don't attend these events then you will miss out on your new opportunity.

With any networking events you have to be careful which one that you attend. Some networking events may be perfect for you and others may not. It depends on your industries or what is your main goal for networking. Some events that you may have to become a member for you actually attending their event. Usually the organizer of that networking event will let you attend one or two events before they will require you to become a paid full pledge member. There are some networking groups will let you attend their event as a non member but you will may have to pay a higher fee and you won't receive the same benefits as a member. There are a lot of benefits when you become a member of a networking group. In some networking group if you become a member and attend the events regularly you may not have to pay a fee because you had already paid your annual dues.

I attended an all-white attire networking event in Bedford Stuyvesant the section of Brooklyn, NY. The networking events were an All White Attire Affair under a tent on Bedford Stuyvesant Restoration Corporation outside grounds. This was given by my friend Donna Jarrett who is the CEO of **"It Takes A Village Today."** It was an awesome event that she had put together. Everybody was dressed in all their white attire. Everybody was in unity and that how networking should be at all time. At that event there were different speakers who were experts in running a successful business on the panels. There were different kinds of entertainment from singers, dancing groups and comedians. We even saw a small skit from a play that was going to be featured on Broadway. There were also a lot of vendors who were selling their products and services. A lot of them were entrepreneurs who are very successful in what they do best. We had also enjoyed the variety of foods and desserts that catered by Chefs and Pastry Chefs who have their own successful business as well. We were there at least half of the day in which it was a beautiful sunny day in the summer. It's very important that you make an effort to connect with the organizer of the event. One time I had even attended a networking event on a cruise that was given by the Hudson County Chamber of Commerce of New Jersey. We took a tour around the Hudson River as well the Hoboken, Jersey City and Bayonne area of New Jersey. I had to purchase a ticket as a non member in the price of $40 for me to attend that event. It was worthy that I had attended that event because again I had made some connections on that cruise boat.

Some people don't like to pay a fee to attend a networking event at all. People just don't realize that the organizer of the networking events has expenses to take care of such as renting of the place, paid for the guest speakers and etc. I usually don't have any problem of paying a fee to attend a networking event because I know that I will get something out of it. I usually find more value in a paying event than a free event. Usually a person that tells me that they don't believe in paying a fee for a networking event, then I know that they really don't want to network. Also they may don't know what networking is really all about. Without question all business has one thing in common and that is a **"Network."** Without network there is no business. On this night our networks will have the chance to **"EXCHANGE"** business cards to one another to build and become stronger as a brand. Unfortunately the brand is not on your business cards but the **"BRAND IS IN YOU"** and we believe if we have more brands in our society today we can grow as a whole.

How to make the most of networking events. Here are some tips that will help you with your experiences at networking events.

- **Networking Events have Different Agenda-** Networking events are common and great opportunities for anyone that believes in networking. There are networking events that have different purposes so you want to make sure that you are attending the right one that will give you the support that you need. For an example if you are in the entertainment industries then you want to attend a networking event that is involved with actors/actresses, singers, producers, musicians and etc. If you are in that field then you will feel more comfortable and you will also follow your purpose in networking. That will definitely be a great way to find new opportunities. Once you make the decisions on which networking events that you want to attend then you need to make your best efforts to achieve the opportunities.

- **Be Prepared-** You need to come prepared when you are attending networking events. You need to bring business cards and plenty of them. It is a serious mistake when you don't bring your business cards at networking events. Your business cards are a little introduction of yourself that leaves with people.

- **Don't Be Late-** You want to get to the event at least 15 minutes before it starts. You will have a greater advantage by arriving early for the networking event because you will have a better opportunity to talk with others who are already there. Also when you are talking to the other guests that they may send you business and opportunities your way. They may also help you with solutions that you were looking for either it is for your business or career.

- **Making Your Best Entrance-** You should enter the room properly like a professional. You should enter the room with a smile on your face. Your entrance should be like you are having a purpose like you are a winner and you take ownership of the room. Nobody doesn't want to deal with someone that has a negative attitude. You should appear in the room like you have some confidence in yourself. Remember that by being confident will attract people. You should definitely try to reach out to the host of the event and thank them for inviting you to their event. If you don't know who is the host of the event you tried to ask someone who is working there point you into their direction. By you getting to know the host then you are starting to build a relationship with them and they also will help you with your networking journey. Also make sure you speak with the staff of the networking group of the events as well the guest speaker.

- **Work on Your Image-** Make sure your images are in part. You should always try to wear professional or business attire. You should try to stay away from jeans unless there are new or dress jeans that you will wear with dress shoes. You should never wear sneakers or slippers to networking events. You also need to make sure that your attire is neat and clean. Your hygiene is also important as well. Make sure that you smell fresh at the event. Nobody doesn't want to smell funky at all. You should always look your best at all times when you are networking.

- **Getting Your Pitch Ready-** Some networking events have an elevator pitch. An elevator pitch is a short introduction that is usually 25words or less about yourself that will describe who you are and what you do. It should not sound like a salesman's pitch in which you are trying to sell your products but it should be specific and explain exactly what you do. Your elevator pitch should be memorable that will be stuck in someone mind. A perfect example is if you are a web designer then you could say that I had designed an application for located different kind of businesses that are owned by African American and Latinos entrepreneurs. That will be a great way to help make your pitch the first good impression and that's all individuals will remember about you when they leave the networking event.

The most important thing to remember is the purpose of attending networking events is to meet people and the process of building relationship. You should never sit by yourself on the side or limit yourself to a few people. You should be able to mingle with many people as possible for the entire event. You need to make an effort to put your focus on each person that you are talking to and make sure that you listen as well. There is an old saying that God given us a mouth to open it to speak and close it to stop talking. God given us ears to listen. When we shut our mouth closed then we are able to listen. There is a time to speak and there is a time to listen. You should not be scared to make small talk. Your purpose is trying to meet new people who you might be able to do business later or work together in the future on a project. When you put your focus on the other person then you are making an attempt to make a great impression at that precious moment. When you are giving out your business cards please make sure that you are doing that with a humble spirit. Putting a smile on your face will also will help in a long way. You should take special note of each card that was handled for you by describing one word about that person. That way you will remember something about that person had caught your attention by their words and actions. It's equally important for you to have their business cards as well in their possession. When someone gives you their business cards that all of their contact information is on that card that you will need to get in contact with them later.

Usually when I am attending networking events I will always meet someone that will tell me that they had forgotten to bring their business cards or they don't have any. They will give me only their email address on a piece of paper. Usually only when somebody gives me their email address that they really telling me that they don't want to network at all or they aren't prepared to network. Again you should always have your business cards with you at all time. If you are running low then you should order more. When it comes to networking you will have to show others that you want to network with others. If somebody does give me a piece of paper with their email address only most likely I will tear that paper up when I get home because what they are really telling me that they don't want to get to know me at all. I sure know from experience because when individuals in the past had done that to me I will still do my follow up by emailing them because that was the only way I could get in contact with them. None of them had never responded to my emails at all so I had just deleted them from my contact list. I had learned my lesson from that experience and just move on. I wasn't going to let that experience to steer me away from networking. It is better to have too many business cards than none at all. That's like going to the supermarket to shop for grocery and you didn't bring any money at all. Without having any means of paying for your grocery the cashier will not let you walk out the supermarket with those groceries. Use that same logic when you are networking. Don't leave home without your business cards. You are a professional so act like one and always be prepared

As the networking event is about to wrap up you need to make sure that you properly said your goodbye to everyone that was at the event. You shouldn't try to sneak out the room without saying goodbye. It is not only professional but it's also shown that you have manner. You should seek out the host and thank him/her again for inviting you to their event. Also while you are doing that you should go around the room and tell them that it was a pleasure of meeting you today. By you doing that you are showing your best impressions to others and they will appreciate it. After the networking event you need to do a follow up. Follow up is really the start of networking. Attending networking events are more like fellowship with other individuals that are attending the event. Networking events may be in themselves intimidating or misleading to some. Calling an event a networking opportunity may create unnecessary stress for individuals that had never network before. In all situations or events that allow you to interact with others will provide the potential for building your network. It is what a person does with the contacts they make at these events that will lead to something closer to their desired outcome.

CHAPTER 3

Going To An Event Doesn't Mean That You Are Networking

"There are two types of people—those who come into a room and say, "Well, here I am! "and those who come in and say, "Ah, there you are." – Frederick Collins

Did you know that by going to a networking event doesn't mean that you are networking? Does your heart race when networking is the crucial part of building up your network for an opportunity? Do you ever feel as if you really belong at a networking event that you attended? Let me tell you that you are not alone at all. When I started to attend networking events, which I really thought I actually was networking. I was busy in pushing sales of my products then realized that I really wasn't networking at all. I really thought of me attending networking events that I was actually networking, but I wasn't at all. Don't get me wrong by attending networking events it is part of the process, but there is a bigger picture. Networking is all about connecting with others and creating those opportunities. You will do this by making an effort to talk to people that you already know and share with them about what you actually do. Also you will introduce yourself to people that you don't know. That's how you are going to connect with new people. That's just like meeting someone for the first time at your favorite place. You even meet people for the first time at a restaurant, library, Starbucks and etc. Networking and building those relationships that are being nurturing are very important to the way businesses and brands are run today.

Some people have fear in meeting new people at a networking event. You don't have to be in fear of meeting new people at the event. For you to be successful at networking events you must have a specific purpose in mind. If you are planning to achieve the mindset of success at the event then you must become very successful at networking. It's up to you how successful you want to be at networking by how well you play the game and the ability to move from one person to the next. And the most important thing that you feel very comfortable was doing just that. A successful networking is just like watching your favorite basketball team playing their best game on ESPN. It May look easy until you tried it for yourself. For some people networking is like getting a long needle in their arm because they are filled with fear and anxiety. The reason that because some of us are in our comfort zone. They feel that they don't know what they should do. For you to feel more comfortable about attending the networking event you can do research about the event. If you like what you see in that research then go ahead and pre-register for the event. If you want even feel more comfortable and safe than bring someone that you know with you in the event that way you won't feel so nervous. Just remember to put a smile on your face and join in with the crowd. Leave your fear of rejection home and just enjoy yourself to network with others. The purpose of networking is to make connections with others. Everybody that attends the event is there to meet new people so don't bring your fear of rejection with you. Understand that networking is a fellowship event that is a friendly and safe environment to meet and greet with others. You should create new connections by exchanging information. There are some individuals who are slightly introverted but you should always go out of your way in networking situations to get other people to talk about themselves. That way you can take that uncomfortable feeling of being the center of attention, what is the great part of doing that you are putting the focus on others instead of constantly talking about yourself. People will be impressed to be around you because of your thinking about others and they will end up loving to do something with you in the future.

Recruiters from different companies will normally be in attendance at these events. It is a great opportunity for them to connect with new clients. The reason why recruiters love to attend networking events is because they know that networking is an awesome way to meet new people and again connect with new prospect clients. They also know the importance of networking in person not just over the phone. That's why it is so important to make an effort to attend networking events because recruiters may show up and may have an opportunity just for you. If you don't show up you will miss your chance with that recruiter who might have a career opportunity for you. I know that sometimes when you go to a place where you don't know anyone can be seem difficult. It may not be a normal surroundings for you but soon or later things do change and believe that it will become easier for you. Networking may be a lot of work but it will become easier. Here is my experience of mastering on networking. If you tried to apply to this information to heart, use it and make an effort by putting it into action at the networking events, then your results may be an improvement in your experience of networking.

- Make sure that you have plenty business cards. When I had attended networking events there are a lot of people do not bring their business cards. Some had even told me that they didn't know that they had supposed to bring business cards.

- If the host/hostess have a nametag with your name on it make sure that you put it on your right side. By shaking your right hand it will bring your name tag into a closer view to that person you are meeting.

- Always arrive on time. By you arriving on time will take away a bit of the stress of the event. You are not going to walk into a large room swarming with people. It will give you a chance to scope the room or get a feel for the room. You will also get a chance to get a bite of appetizers and drinks before the event get too busy.

- Bring a friend that can become your network buddy who is in another industry if possible. At least it will take the stress of going by yourself. There is always strength in numbers. Do not spend the entire time there with your friend. The purpose for you to network is to connect with people who you don't know. Your friend can mingle with others so he/she can meet a new connection. That's the purpose of the event is to meet new people.

- Have a secret pact that your friend will recognize. Like this example if someone that you are having a conversation with won't let you out of their conversation then you use your secret code to let your friend know that you need their help to come your rescue by politely take you away from that conversation. You can also say excuse me but I must talk with the guest speaker about something. This great way of escape for you to avoid that long dreary long conversation with that person so you can mingle with others.

- Tried to go to events other than events for people who do what you do. For example if you sell Financial Products such as Mutual Funds and Money Markets Funds then it won't make sense to go to another financial company networking event. Instead tried to go to a community First Home Buyers Workshop Seminar that is another great way of connecting with new people. Those new connections can become your new prospect client.

- You should take the opportunity to be the first to introduce yourself to others. If you wait for someone to approach you then you might spend the entire event alone and you will feel miserable. You will also miss out on new connections.

- You should work on your elevator speech about by thirty to forty seconds at the most. You can say that you are a writer, consultant, motivational speaker who works with organizations to develop growth in different areas. If they want to hear more than you can answer their questions. You should not give them a 30 minute lecture at all.

- To ease the relationship and set a tone of mutual interest you should ask the other person first what they do. They will really appreciate it. I know that I definitely will.

- You should not spend no more than 10 to 12 minutes with each individual. The best way to excuse yourself from a conversation is to say something. This I would have said to someone **"I am really glad we had a chance to talk. I see Mr. Washington across the room and if I don't talk to him, he will not forgive me."** Just shake their hands, look into their eyes, give them a smile and move forward to the next person.

- You can talk about anything other than what you do in your industry. I like to talk about my hobbies such as music and sports. The conversation will be more interesting because you may find out that the both of you may have the same thing in common. The relationship is more important in blossom than trying to impress someone of what you do.

- In the world of networking events there are two types of people, guests and hosts. Guests always like to be taken care of and a great host will like to take care of others. If you are attending a networking event and if you see that something can be more successful at that event you can always volunteer your service by helping out. You can even stay always to the end and help the host and staffs to clean up and pack everything away so the place will be nice and neat. The host of the event will definitely remember your kind service that you had offered. Also you will help them to be able to rent that place for their next event. I know what I am talking about because I had done that myself. You should never sell at a networking event. It is not for that purpose at all. You don't want to make anyone feel uncomfortable.

- You should never make a promise to that person you will give them a call and not follow through. Nobody like a broken promise. People are like music. Some will tell you the truth while others are just making loud noise. Your action will speaks for itself.

- Just in case someone snubs you or ignore you the best thing is just move on. That is their loss not yours. This usually happens because they are miserable, unprepared and very insecure. You should not take that personally at all.

- If you are in the middle of talking with someone and somebody else is waiting patiently and politely at the side for the right moment to make an introduction to you just invite that person to join in your conversation. This is a meet and greet event. The more that join in your conversation the better it will be for you to get even more connections.

- You should always bring your best people skills and your

best manners at networking events. You will definitely going to need them. Remember this is a professional event and you are going to be surrounded with professionals and entrepreneurs. You should always be on your best behavior. Nobody doesn't want to be around with someone that is very rule or don't have any class at all.

Keep all of this great information that I had shared with you in mind. You are off to a great start by having a better time of networking than you suspect. You can achieve great results in meeting new connections if you work your magic by keeping on putting the work in your networking. Personally you should be able to try to do one networking event per week. Attending two networking events per week is even better on your part. By you starting to attend networking events can lead you to expand your own network. This can only help you when the time comes to pick up your phone. When you do that you will get the help, advice, support or that introduction that you were looking for.

"The successful networkers I know, the ones receiving tons of referrals and feeling truly happy about themselves, continually put the other person's needs ahead of their own." ~~Bob Burg

CHAPTER 4

Beyond The Networking Events

"The way of the world is meeting people through other people."~~Robert Kerrigan

Networking events aren't the only place that you can go to for you to network. You can do your networking at most of your favorite places. If you are used to start a conversation with someone that you hadn't met before then you will be able to start to expand your network. Johan Arndt has a quote about conversations **"Informal conversation is probably the oldest mechanism by which opinions on products and brands are developed, expressed, and spread."** When we even start to hold a conversation with someone we don't realize that we are capable to network with each other. Networking is like going to fellowship with one another. Again you should not limit yourself to network by only going to networking events. There are so many different places that you can network at. You can network with your family members, friends, classmates, coworkers, fellow church members and etc.

The Churches are the best examples when it comes to networking. They spend a lot of time of fellowship with one another. They don't only fellowship with their own members but they will go out and fellowship with other churches. When a Church has their Anniversary either it is of the Church or Pastor they always end up inviting a guest speaker. In most cases the guest speaker even brings their Choirs and congregation with them. The best part those churches are building personal relationship with each other's. They support each other well. Same with the Church and Community Choirs. When these choirs are having functions such as Concerts or anniversary they usually invite guest choirs to sing at their event. Those Choirs always looking forward to fellowship with other choirs. They enjoy the fellowship with each other. They will go and support each other well. These Choirs will build relationships with other choirs. These Churches and Choirs know that if they only want their guests comes to them but if they don't return the favor, then they know that they had broken the fellowship. Like I tell people all the time that support goes both ways, not one way. People are willing to work with you but you have to make an effort to work with the others. Bob Burg has mentioned a quote about putting other peoples' needs over your own, **"The successful networkers I know, the ones receiving tons of referrals and feeling truly happy about themselves, continually put the other person's needs ahead of their own."**

Another great place to network is always at seminars and conventions. Conventions are definitely perfect to network with because you will meet different tons of people. I will use the Gospel Music Workshop of America National Convention **(GMWA)** as a perfect example. GMWA have their annual national conventions every year in the summer time in different Cities. GMWA had been around almost 50 years in which the convention was started by Reverend James Cleveland in Detroit, MI. The reverend Cleveland purpose of starting this convention was to unite Gospel Artists, Groups and Choirs united together. There are Chapters in different States. The Choir directors, musicians, soloists, Choirs, Churches, Ministers and etc. All attend this convention to make connections. They know how to network really well. A lot of them attend this convention because they know that recording companies and producers will be down there to discover new talents. Even the Preachers network at these conventions as well by making new connections and building new relationships. They are looking for new fellowships for their churches with other congregations.

If you are a member of a Church then you can always network with your fellow members. Since you carry a membership at that Church then most likely they may already know you by participating activities that are going on at the Church. Don't be afraid to communicate with your fellow members. In matter fact the Church should be a place to help give their support to members who are in need either a job placement or help with their business. There are a lot of business owners who are members at Church. The Churches need to start supporting their own fellow members that have their own business. They can be a blessing to their fellow church members' business. Also if they give you great services then you should give them referrals as well. Share your resources with others. We as the church need to learn to create our own economy and wealth by supporting our fellow members who have their own business.

The Chamber of Commerce in your surrounding area could be another great way to network with. The Chamber of Commerce is the world's largest business organization representing the interests of more than 3 million businesses of all sizes, sectors, and regions. The members of the U.S. Chamber of Commerce range from mom-and-pops stores and local chambers to leading industry associations and large corporations. They all share one thing in common. They all count on the Chamber of Commerce to be their voice in Washington, D.C. They have some many resources that you can benefit from. By being part of the Chamber of Commerce you can reap the benefits of becoming a member. The Chamber of Commerce is always having different kind of events and they have professionals from all different kinds of sectors that you can connect with. They can lead you to the right connection that you need. They also can lead you to organizations that they are in partnership with to help you out with your opportunity that you are looking for. The most important thing that you can do is to meet with the person who is in charge of The Chamber of Commerce in your area and see if they can tell you information about their organization to help you decide to join. They will also be the best person you can network with as well. Your favorite gym is another place where you can network with. This is the place where people have their workout in and usually the place where you are always meeting new people at. I had met some great friends at the gym where I work out at. You will have a chance to talk with your new connection after your workout at the gym maybe for lunch or coffee for you two to get to know each other. You will both learn something about each other. As you talk regularly to that person you are starting to build a relationship. Just remember that networking is all about building solid relationship.

You can even network with your favorite Fraternities and Sororities. Fraternities and Sororities such as the Alpha Phi Alpha Fraternity and The Delta Phi Fraternity are great organizations to network with. One thing about all of these Fraternities and Sororities that you are a part of something great. To be involved with these organizations it will require you to have a membership with them. By you are part of them you will have a better chance to meet a lot of new connections. These organizations stay in contact with their members even after they had finished their college education. With these Fraternities and Sororities that they are always having different kinds of function each year. They actually look out for their members. As a member you can go to your fellow members for help anything that you may need such as a career or support with your business. The network is a separate word that equals to **'Net Work'** reminds us of the vital aspects of modern successful networking, by which ideally:

We work (apply thought, commitment, effort)

To **create**, grow, use, assist and enable

Our own **net (network)** of contacts.

To have a good network you must create a good network that networking will succeed by the application of your hard work. If you have a network without the hard work then your network will produce nothing worthwhile. You must create your own opportunity to network.

I mentioned about the Choirs earlier in this chapter. If you are a faithful member that sings in a Choir then you should be able to network with your fellow Choir members. The Choir rather it is a Church or Community Choir is the best way of networking because you will always have a chance to make new connections. Choir members know a lot of people and they have strong connections that you need to meet in their circle. Don't be afraid to connect with your fellow choir members. Just like when you are singing in the Choir with harmony, networking is all about being in harmony or be united. To get that perfect sound the Choir must sing in harmony. To have a successful networking experience you must be willing to be in harmony with others regardless where you network at. The purpose of networking is working as a team. We as Networker use a network of professional or social contacts to further our career. Networking is all about being social and able to communicate with others. Networking is also about to Interact with others to exchange information and develop professional or social contacts.

A lot of people feel that they can't network with someone that they already met, but you can network with someone that you already know. Even if you knew that person for a long time. I met up with one of my good friends Carl June and I have known him over 10 years. We had met up in the city and we had network together after work. I had also network with my friend Eula Guest who is the owner of Girot's Roll Film Production. I have known her since early 2010 at the Black Business Works Networking Event. I went to some of her functions that she organized to give her my support. Also she is willing to help promote others without expecting anything in return. You should never feel that you can't network because you already know that person. That person that you already know can be a blessing to you by helping you with a better opportunity for yourself. They can lead you to their best connections that you couldn't reach them on your own. Some will lose out on their blessing of opportunities because they are busy judging the person by their book cover on the outside. You can't judge someone from the outside of their book cover but the inside of the book.

Chapter 5

Business Network

"The richest people in the world look for and build networks, everyone else looks for work." Robert Kiyosaki

In the business community today entrepreneurs need to network with other business owners and professionals. It is very important to have the ability to network successfully to have the one of the greatest assets in the business community. Networking will allow some individuals to find great opportunities while others will watch from the sidelines. To have an effective networking experience you must be willing to work hard and be persistent. Effective networking shouldn't be about a result of luck. Here what it takes to have a great effective networking experience. Here are the seven important traits of habits to achieve:

- **(Make sure that you ask questions)** Before you make an attempt to attend networking events you should try to find out who will be attending and search Social Media sites like Facebook and LinkedIn to see what the topics are going to be discussed. You should also get to know the people in your network. Find out what assistance does they need help in. Ask to see what they are working on right now. By you are getting to know that person in your network that you are starting the process of building a solid foundation of relationship. Planning a one on one meeting either at lunch or dinner.

- **(Adds Some Value)** The most outcomes of powerful practices are to present some value to your new connection. You will help out by finding a way to help someone take action. If you know that someone can use the help with a new connection with a situation then you need to drop what you are doing and make an effort to provide an introduction for the two individuals to meet. We all need help with meeting new connections and we will want that help. So treat the person the same way that you wanted to be treated. *"The currency of real networking is not greed but generosity." By* **Keith Ferrazzi**

- **(Learn Their History)** You should ask entrepreneurs that are very successful in their crafts to share with you their story on how they had started as an entrepreneur. You are building rapport by listening to their stories about how they became successful. By listening to their stories and by you showing an interest in their history that you can learn from their approach in the business world. The more that you understand that person in your network the better you can add and attract value from that relationship you are building. *"If you want to go somewhere, it is best to find someone who has already been there." By* **Robert Kiyosaki**

- **(Share A Memorable Moment)** When a person that you had met the first time asks you the question **"What You Do?"** don't give a long stretch story about your business and career. Instead mention something personal that really defines you. Describe your hobbies like music and arts that may show the other person about your passion. They may just have the same thing in common with you. By you sharing your personal passion that can help brighten the mood and get individuals join in the conversation. *"A friendship founded on business is better than a business founded on friendship." By* **John D. Rockefeller**

- **(Make A List)** What is your mission after attending a networking event or meal? If your mission is, **"Should I go home,"** you're probably going to miss out on those opportunities. Write down important topics that was mention of the event. This habit can help prevent opportunities from falling through the mud and will give you something to bring up in a conversation the next time you meet up. You can also develop a reputation as someone who's on top of your game. *"Position yourself as a center of influence, the one who knows the movers and shakers. People will respond to that, and you'll soon become what you project." By* **Bob Burg**

- **(Making that promise and stand by your word)** No matter what kind of promise that you had made such as sending an email or returning a phone call. Please deliver on your promise.

That promise that you had just made will reflects on your own character. Like my favorite sayings Talk is cheap so show me by your action. By following through on your word, you start building a reputation for trustworthiness, which is exactly how every great Networker wants to be perceived by. *"It's all about people. It's about networking and being nice to people and not burning any bridges." By* **Mike Davidson**

- **Reward Your New Connection-** You should keep a list of your new connections that stay in contact with you. Each week you should do something special to add value to one person's life or business. You might send them a book or set up a lunch date to introduce them to one of your other connections. This kindness of value can help you be more proactive about staying in touch with your most powerful connections. Just as with fitness or investing, the most successful people are the ones who choose to be consistent in their own actions. **"Your Actions Will Define Your Character."**

These are the successful ways of having effective networking experiences. The more that you network you will become an expert in effective networking. In the business networking community that can be great as a support by working together. It doesn't always have to be about a competition thing. When you make an effort to network with Local Business Owners then you can do the following:

- **(Find Potential Partnership within the Business Community)** When you are making an effort to reach out to those local business owners then you may find convenient a possibility business partner that you can team up with for events, projects, to share clients with, to participate in joint ventures, and to share support with each other. For example, non-competing business owners such as a restaurant and a bakery can team up and agree to refer clients to each other in a deal that will benefit both of their businesses and their customers! Like a restaurant owner who don't have experience in baking desserts can work with a baker by ordering desserts from him/her such as cakes and pies. To that baker who needs to have food catered at an event that he/she may be involved in can hire that particular restaurant for a catering job. They can also refer business to each others.

- **(Increase Your Connections in the Local Business Community)** Find that local business owners in your business community that may have existing connections with other business owners, suppliers, or clients that may benefit your own business. Each new connection with business owners may provide links to other valuable contacts that you may not have had access to at all. It really is great to get involved in that merchant association in your local business community where your businesses are in. You will have better opportunity to network and work together in harmony. **"We are only as strong as we are united, as weak as we are divided." By J.K. Rowling,**

- **(Generate credibility to you and your Business)** By you taking the advantage of networking with local business owners you will be able to generate more visibility and credibility for you and your business in your local community. Your new found visibility and credibility makes it easier for you to be selected by other business owners who may want to form a possibility partner with businesses in your industry. Also by you are getting involved with the local community that your business is in then that community will get to know you and they will build a relationship with you and your business.

- **(Finding That Experienced Mentors in Business)** By you taking the opportunity of networking with local business owners then you will be able to find more experienced entrepreneurs who are willing to mentor you. Since you are making connections with a mentor in your local business community then they can share you some wisdom, information and tips about resources and clients. These mentors are the great resources for help because they can share you their good and bad experiences in running their business. Their experiences are some great learning experiences

- **(Grow a Local and Support Networks)** As you take on the role of a business owner there will be times when you need to get advice and support from fellow local business owner about issues related to your local area or industry. You will definitely want to meet in person with other business owners in your network. When you are working with other business owners in your local community or network you are giving each other support. Support goes both ways. You can find these local businesses online or on social Media site such as Facebook and Linkedin. You now have the access to the better of different ways of having support when you are networking with other business owners.

That's the way as an Entrepreneur that you network with your local business community. You are actually building a solid relationship within your local business community.

I want to also mention about Network Marketing Companies or MLM companies in this chapter. A person who is an affiliate of a network marketing company can also benefit from networking. You are asking me **"What are Network Marketing Companies?"** The answer is that is a method of marketing that utilizes independent representatives to reach potential customers that a company otherwise would not reach traditional online or offline marketing methods. Networking Marketing Companies want access to your network that includes your friends and family members. There are so many companies that are offering products and services. A lot of them you may recognize by their brand name. There are products and services that these companies will let you market will cover from Communications to Financial Services. They need to recruit people because these companies don't believe in paying tons of money for advertisements instead they will use the word of mouth marketing tools that is more powerful and effective method of marketing. That's especially effective when that message comes from someone that we already know and trust. *"If you are a person with big dreams and would love to support others in achieving their big dreams, then the network marketing business is definitely a business for you. You can start your business part-time at first and then as your business grows, you can help other people start their part-time business. This is a value worth having – a business and people who help others make their dreams come true."* **By Robert Kiyosaki**

I attended so many networking events and at most of them you will see someone from a network marketing company. They think that they are networking by trying to recruit you for their company at the event. When you are attending those events you should not be trying to sell your products or trying to recruit someone. People will get turned off real quick. One time this guy came to talk to me at a networking event so we had made an introduction to each other. At that time I was working with a network marketing company that is a financial services company. He already knew I was already working with a MLM Company and all he was interested in was to recruit me to his network marketing company. I told him that I can't work for his company because it will be a conflict of interest. He was so angry with me and bashes the company. I was so turned off that I just walked away from him. You should never bash any company when you are networking. The purpose for you to attend these events to meet new connections and start the process of building relationship by getting to know each other. A lot of these guys do not know how to build relationships. They will not even call you at all. Another person told me to call him only when I am ready to join his network marketing company. After that I just torn up his business card.

People who work with network marketing company should be able to network well since the business that they are in require them to communicate with people for their business to survive. When you start to exchange business cards the first thing you should make an introduction then find out something about that person. You start to get to know that person. When you are networking just like everybody else your focus should be starting to build new relationships. After you get to know that person and build that relationship then you can start to talk about what you really do. If you want that person to buy your product or services then you need to support them as well. Support goes both ways and not one way. A woman called me one afternoon that I met at a networking event. She supposed to do a follow up call, but her purpose was to get my friend John number and address so she can push her product to him. I told her that I couldn't give you his information without his permission. She told me don't be stupid. I told her you are starting to be rude and I need to hang up on you because you aren't being professional. She also mentioned that she doesn't believe that support goes both ways. I didn't want to network with her because she was a waste of my time and energy. She tried to call me again but I ignored her call. Again when you are networking with someone you should always be on your best behavior at all time. You never know who you might meet. Even though a lot of people weren't doing business with me when I was with Primerica, but I stay in contact with them. Now that I am an Author that those people that I established relationship with are now a blessing to me in my new opportunity.

"Most business people think they know how to network; they might be great at mingling, but don't take the necessary steps to turn introductions into prospects."~~Mike Sullivan

CHAPTER 6

NETWORKING ON SOCIAL MEDIA

"Social networking sites like MySpace, Friendster, and Facebook have literally exploded in popularity in just a few short years." ~~Mike Fitzpatrick

Social Media such as Facebook and Linkedin are other great ways to network. There are different ways on how you can do your networking with Social Media. Social Media is an awesome way of meeting new connections. You can meet your new prospect connections on Social Media either individually or Groups that are on that Social Media Sites. Facebook, Linkedin, Google Plus and others have groups that might cater to your needs or interests. There are so many groups you can join such as Business, Music, Churches, Motivational Groups and etc. If you join these groups you need to participate regularly so you can get to know at least some of the members. Personally that was how I was able to make new connections by joining some of these groups. Daily I will post Quotes on the group walls. I also like the post that other members in the group had posted and responded to their comments. Some of those members had personally asked me to become friends with them on Facebook and Linkedin. This could be another great way to grow your network. You get to know your new connections from Social Media by starting to build a relationship with them. You take the time out by talking regularly by chat, emails and eventually on the phone. Soon or later you can't hide behind Social Media because eventually you need to take courage of meeting them in person.

Social Media such as Linkedin and Facebook is a great way to network with others. It is a great tool for new connections. Those new people that you had just met on Facebook and Linkedin will try to do whatever they can to help their connections in your networking efforts. They can be a piece in the puzzles as you network to find employment, grow your business, hire talent, share best practices with each other's, ask plenty questions, willing to learn, share knowledge with others, reconnect with former coworkers and finding new opportunities. Keep in mind that with a large network there is a lot of effort and a big investment but it is all worth at the end. What goes around does come around because that is when you are a blessing to others by helping with your knowledge and your connections then most likely they will reciprocate the same efforts to you. There are several requests that cross the line. People should remember to leverage their network without taking advantage of it. Here are the most common Facebook and Linkedin networking mistakes that I experienced for myself:

What Not to Do while networking on Social Media like Facebook and Linkedin?

1. Can You Endorse Me?

Lots of us are open to network with others, meeting up with new professionals and connecting with them for mutual networking purposes. My purpose to network is to build solid relationships. I want to help you to network and I will do my best as I can. If I have never met you before or haven't any interaction with you yet, then please don't ask me to endorse you, write a recommendation or refer my connections to you. I need to get to know you better by us building a relationship with each other's. My endorsement should mean more than that. That's Real Talk!

2. Can You Give Me a Job?

I hate to bust your bubble, but I can't give you a job. A recruiter is someone who finds candidates to fill jobs. Their job is not to find jobs to employ candidates. A lot of people make that mistake. I am not a recruiter but I will be happy to refer you to a recruiter or my connection for a job. Again I can't give you a job or make somebody to give you a job. You are the one have to put the work in.

3. Can You send me John Doe's Phone Number

If people wanted their phone number to be public knowledge, they'd put it right on their profile **(and many of them do, so please check there first!)**. If not, then it's really not my place to give out their phone numbers to others. Instead let me get their permission first if it's okay for me to pass their phone number to you. If they give me their permission then I will be gladly to pass their phone number to you. Otherwise I am not giving you their phone number.

4. Try to recruit people in their Networking Marketing Business

There been many times that people requested to connect with me on Facebook or Linkedin in the purpose to recruit me in their networking business. You should not be asking someone to join your network marketing business since you just connected with them on Facebook and Linkedin. You should be trying to build a relationship with your new connections. If you found out that your new connection is already involved in a network marketing company, then you should not be asking them to get involved with yours. They can only do one at a time. The purpose of a network marketing company is to recruit individuals to help the company to grow by building a team, make the company money and want individuals to be loyal to their company.

5. Asking a professional "Do they know of any job openings that fit my profile?"

Rather than coming to a professional with such an open-ended question and having done no research at all on your part then expecting a professional to do all of the homework. You need to make some effort and do some legwork ahead of time. If that professional you had asks that question who is a recruiter then you need to read their profile. You should realize that they are only a recruiter for that one company. Secondly you should make the time to visit the company's career page and apply online then come to that recruiter or that connection with some specific positions of interest in mind. I am very sure that they will be gladly done what they can to put you in touch with the appropriate decision makers. By doing your homework on your end will not only speed up the process, but it will also put less of a burden on the professional you are asking for help.

6. Can You Please Send Me John Doe's Email Address?

I am very sure that if people had wanted their email address to be public knowledge then they would have put it right on their Facebook or Linkedin Profile. Just like in **example #3(Phone Numbers)** many of them does put it on their profile then you should check there. If it is not then it is not really my place to give out their email address to others so don't waste my time to ask me. First I need to get their permission to give you their email address. I will be honored to pass along your introduction request to them on your behalf and it's up to them if they will like to follow up with you or not.

7. <u>Do you know anyone at Morgan Stanley?</u>

Maybe! In most likely that I probably know (or am connected to) dozens of people at Morgan Stanley. Just because I used to work at that particular company doesn't mean I can give you a job there. You need to take the time to do your own research and homework. Also if you hadn't made any attempt to build a relationship with me then don't expect me to help you in your time of needs. You can easily find out the answers that you need. Then after that you can send me a personal introduction request or perhaps someone else in your network who can introduce you to the perfect target contact. You are the only one know the reason why you want to reach out and who the best contact person at that particular company might be.

8. <u>Can You Please Check Out My Resume and give me your feedback/Any Suggestions?</u>

I will love to help, but I am not a resume expert. I have a problem with my own resume and that's why I get a professional to do mines that have an expertise in resume writing. Resume writing is a very time intensive process that requires a two way discussion, extensive editing and re-writing, spell checking and grammars. Professional Resume Writers do charge big bucks for their services because they are experts in writing a resume and it's not an easy task at all. Again I am not an expert so it is the best to go to a professional resume writer.

9. <u>I don't want to make any effort to meet up with you</u>

Often times when someone wants to connect with you either on Facebook or Linkedin they only want add you to their connection list online to get a certain amount of connections. They don't want to make an effort to get to know you or building relationship with you. The purpose of connecting with those social media is for networking. Part of networking is communications. Eventually you are going to need to chat with that person on the phone. You are going to need to make an attempt to meet that connection in person. Meeting up for coffee, lunch or dinner is a great way of getting to know each other and building solid relationship. That's how I had gained my great knowledge of networking. Also I had met a lot of new connections because I had put the work in to network with others. Without communication you are not going to have a successful networking experience. If you don't have any desire to communicate with anyone then you are wasting your time and you shouldn't be networking at all. You have to make the time to network with others. Regardless of how busy your schedules are you need to make the time in building solid relationship with others.

10. <u>Hi Melvin/Hi Brother/Hi {First Name} / Hi Special Friend/ Hi Sean John</u>

When reaching out to contacts on Linkedin or Facebook you need to make sure that you have their name right. **"Melvin"** is close (**but still wrong**), **"Brother"** that is not my name at all and I am not your brother. **What's Up Sean John?** My name is not **Sean John**. I had people called me Sean John because they think that I look like him. I am not Sean John and there is only one Sean John Combs. That's the quickest way to turn me off and your recipient. On a personal note, please get their name right. My name is Milton and I want to be called by that name. If I could get your name right then I expect the same from you. **That's Respect!**

11. <u>I Love Your Picture On Linkedin and Facebook. Let's Hook Up and Go Out On A Date.</u>

Linkedin is a professional networking site, not a dating site. My Facebook Page is a professional page just like Linkedin. People send me request to friend them on Facebook and connect with them on Linkedin for the purpose of dating me. Some of their profile pictures have no clothes on at all. If it is not for networking or business purpose then I will not friend you on Facebook. Also if I decide to friend you and you cross the line then I am not only unfriend you but I will push the block button. Word of advice from me: please refrain from trying to **"pick up"** your connections or asking them out on a date. Also please don't come across as a stalker. When you start to do that then it's my pleasure to go to my immediate trip to my **"Remove Connections"** and **"The Block Button"** from my page. Believe me I don't have any problem doing that.

So please follow the common rules of the rules of networking on Social Media. Also you want to be on your best behavior at all time. People are watching you at all times on Social Media like Facebook and Google Plus. You should be professional at all times. Using Linkedin site you don't have any choice but be professional. If you posted naked pictures of yourself or you being drunk they will cancel your account.

Recently a person sent me a friend request on Facebook. I accepted the request because since he is a fellow author that I wanted to network with him. The next day that I was on Facebook to promote my books he started to chat with me on Facebook. He asked me questions about my books. Then he asked me this question **"Would you like to interview with me on my blog talking about your books?"** I told him sure I will like that. Then the next thing he mentioned to me **"You didn't ask me how much that you have to pay me for the interview."** I told him that when somebody is giving me an opportunity to help me to promote my books on their blog or on their radio show, I will say thank you and show how grateful that I am. He then asked me **"Even if you have to pay for the interview?"** I told him that usually that person will tell you up front if you have to pay a fee for the interview. He then mentioned that **"Milton, you are a very smart guy. I will tell you what I will interview you tomorrow for free but don't tell anyone."** I told him that I am on Facebook to network with my fellow authors and professionals. I am also here to build relationships as well. He then tells me "That's great and keep on networking but make money on Facebook from your Facebook friends. I was so turned off from him that I shut down my Facebook page. The next day I log onto Facebook and soon that I was with this person tried to chat with me. I ignored him and log off from Facebook. My advice to you is when somebody accepts your friend request please don't start to sell your product to them. That's a big turn off and people will be pissed off with you. You need to get to know them first by starting to build relationships with them.

Let me get back into groups on Facebook and Linkedin. Personally I think it is great to be involved with groups on Social Media that have a moderator who is going to keep the topic going. Like I have a group on Facebook **"Create Your Own Opportunity Network Group"** in which I will post something positive or information on the page. I even encourage the members to respond and even post their own information as well as long it is going to empower the members. Some groups on Facebook will not let you post anything on their page so I don't waste my time to be involved in that group because I am not going to benefit from that. When I join these groups either on Facebook, Linkedin, Google Plus and others that for the purpose to network with others. I created the opportunity to meet a lot of new connections by going that route and now I am building solid relationships with them.

I am an Author and there are special Social Media sites just for Authors and Publishers. I am part of Author Den, Black Author Connect and others. What I like about these sites is that there is no competition at all. There is a lot of support from fellow Authors. They will share their knowledge and experiences with you to help you with your success as an author. They will give you a lot of resources and tools such as the choices for you to choose from as going to a traditional publisher or having your book self-publish. Since I had published my book "Walking In God's Path Toward Your Destination Volume 1" To Change Your Mindset that some fellow Authors had shared the information about my book to their network. My friend Elois Thames who is an Author and Owner of Rare Diamond Publication of Flint, Michigan interviewed me on her Company Blog. For the whole week she made sure that my book was feature on her blog page and encouraging her readers to purchase my book. If I didn't network with her on Facebook Group that we both belong to I would have missed my opportunity to promote my book. Another way that I meet new connections from a Group on Facebook or Linkedin is like their post and response to their post. Then I will start a conversation with them.

Since I started to network with many authors on different Social Media sites that I was able to take my books to the next level. A lot of my new connections that I met was on marketing website for authors. A lot of them have blogs in which I decided to follow. I have a lot of followers on my blogs as well. Blogs are another way that you can network with others. I made several new connections that way. I already have new opportunities coming my way because I am willing to take the necessary steps to network in different ways for in the purpose of meeting new connections.

Milton Kelly

Chapter 7

The Follow Up

"Honestly networking is a waste of time and effort for most people simply because they don't do 1 thing… follow up . Or they follow up in a way that is counterproductive and leads to loss of trust.~~Patrick Powers

The most important part of networking is the follow up. That's when the real networking starts when you do the follow up. A lot of people that goes to networking events don't have a clue about the importance of the follow up. The purpose of doing the follow up is to start the process of building solid relationships with your potential new connections. When I am networking I make sure when I am collecting individual business cards that I make sure I take the time to do the follow up. Soon the networking events are over I make sure I start the follow up soon several hours later or the next day. I don't wait for the person to do the follow up with me, I will lead the task to do the follow up. Networking really do not start at the networking events but networking actually starts with the follow up. Some individuals have a misunderstanding about networking concept. The development of building a strong network requires making those connections that will sustain more than an introduction. To develop a strong network you need the ingredients of those connections and the support that are requiring maintaining them. An initial meeting or contact with someone does not establish a connection unless you make an effort to do your follow-up of some kind. The follow-up must suggest a mutual interest in developing a meaningful supportive relationship.

Oftentimes when I meet individuals at networking events they don't have a clue about networking. They figure that just because they are attending a networking event that they are networking. Patrick Powers have mentioned that **"Honestly networking is a waste of time and effort for most people simply because they don't do the one thing and that's the follow up."** You must do the follow up because that is the most important factor of networking. I went to so many networking events and after the events were over that most people I will never hear from them. I will make sure that I do all of my follow up immediately after the networking events are over. Some will get back to me while others will never get back to me. Your purpose of networking will be a waste of your time if you don't make an effort of doing your follow up. Some people will wait for others to get in contact with them. If the person that they had met don't get in contact with them then they won't make an effort to do the follow up.

Also some people that do their follow up ends up doing it the wrong way. They will start to try to sell you something or get involved in their network marketing business opportunity. Follow up is about to get to know your new connections in the purpose of building relationship. What is building relationship all about? Relationships are the building blocks for all walks of life. Building relationships are for achieving goals of working together as a team. When you are part of a team you will never see one person working alone. When you are part of a team that you are working together in unity. Building relationships are the foundation of an organized effort for change. We all need lots of people to contribute their ideas, take a stand and get the job done. Building relationships can also be part of a community that will motivate us to reach our goals and care for one another. Building that solid relationships don't have any room of being selfish. Building relationships is all about the foundation of trust. Trust is very important in building solid relationships. I don't care what kind of relationships if it is personal or professionals there have to be trust in the equations.

If you don't do your follow up then your effort of networking will not work out for you at all. Networking will rarely works after meeting that person only at the networking event. Networking is all about building trust from each other's. You will never really trust somebody after only meeting them only one time. You will have to get to know the person by making an effort to build a solid relationship. It is just like you meet somebody that you will like to date. You will not marry that person after that first date. Wouldn't You? If you do then you are crazy for doing that. It is a process of getting to know everything about each other's. In most cases after several days that person isn't going to remember you unless you do your follow up. A lot of people have a misunderstanding of the purpose of doing the follow up and of networking. Some will not do a follow up because either they don't believe it or they just don't know. One thing I can say when I was with Primerica that we have to do some prospecting or recruiting and the individuals that we had met. After we had met we will exchange phone numbers and we will have to do a follow up calls to get to know our prospects. We start to try to build relationship by getting to know them. After we learn something about them we will try to invite them to an opportunity meeting to show what we do. After they attend one of our opportunity meetings we will check up on them by making a follow up call. Some will join the company and others will want to do business with us. Then there are some will not have an interest in nothing what we have to offer but the most important thing is that without making those phone calls you will not have succeeded in your business. I had noticed personally for myself that some people will do their follow up with me being so pushy and judgmental. It was a guy that I met a networking event and we exchange our contact information. Later on at the event he was trashing the company that I was working with and say that his Financial Services Company was better. Then when he had done his follow up with me that he was very rude with me. After I had told him who I was and what I did at that time. He had said to me I didn't mean to call you and then he asked me about my educations. After he mentioned that I will have to think about networking with you. I told him don't bother at all. You are the type of person that I don't want to deal with. You don't want to build a relationship. I tore up his business cards. When you do your follow up you need to be professional at all time. You should never judge someone because that person can be a blessing to your personal life or professional life.

There are different ways that you can do your follow up after an event. You can do your follow up by letters, emails, faxes, phone calls and even on Social Media like Facebook and Linkedin. After every networking event I will get in contact with you either by a phone call, emails or connecting with you on Facebook and Linkedin. In most cases the new prospect connections that I had met at the networking events that I invite them to connect on Facebook will accept my friend request on Facebook. It's even better on Linkedin as well. Once you have sent a request to connect on Linkedin then most likely they will accept your request to connect with you on Linkedin. After they accept my friend request on Facebook or Linkedin I will send them a thank you note for accepting my invitations to be my connections. They will really appreciate that you took time out for your gratefulness of them accepting you.

By you doing your follow up you are starting the process of building relationships. Here are ways that you have a successful experience of building solid relationships:

You need to build relationships one at a time. Dean Witter had a quote as their motto **"We measure success one investor at a time."**This also goes for building relationships as well. There are no short cuts when you are building relationships. It takes a lot of work in getting to know the person. That is the process of relationship builder.

You need to make an effort to be friendly and willing to make a connection. A friendly word or smile can make somebody's day. You should try to find something in common. We all want to have close connections with others

You should ask questions. People always love to talk about themselves and what they are thinking about. If you join in the conversation and ask people to describe themselves. While they are telling you about themselves you should take the time to listen with care then they will become friends with you.

Make sure you tell people about yourself. People are willing to trust you if you take the time out to trust them. Just tell them what you care about and what's on your mind.

You need to go places and do things together. If you want to make friends then you need to share your time with them like attending picnics, movies, conferences, concerts, dinner, lunch and etc. Part of the follow up after networking is that you have to take the time to meet with your connections in person.

You just need to accept people the way they are. You don't always have to agree with them in order for you to form that solid relationship. You should not judge anyone because you wouldn't want someone to judge you.

You should assume that the other person wants to build a relationship as well. Some people did look like they aren't friendly but they are just shy. Deep down they want somebody to talk with them.

 You need to overcome your fear of rejection. Most of us are dealing with fear of rejection including me. The best thing for us to do is just get over it. If you want to create some kind of relationship then you need to expect to be rejected sometimes. That's part of life. You will be blessed the rest of the time with the new relationship that you had started.

You need to be persistent. People are often shy and don't trust anyone. It will take time to form a relationship if you take the time to stick with. A good relationship doesn't just happen overnight.

You should just make an effort to invite people to get involved. People want to become part of something by doing something to benefit others than themselves. Many people are looking for different ways of opportunity to meet other people that share common interests. Most people will be honored that you had invited them.

You should enjoy being in the company of people. If you enjoy being around people then others will be attracted to your attitude. People will definitely want to be around your company.

These are the steps that you can follow the steps in building wonderful relationships regardless of what kind it is.

When you are doing your follow up, you should ask your new connections to meet in person for coffee, breakfast, lunch or dinner. You can also meet in public places like the parks, basketball game or just sitting on a bench or on a stoop. Part of building relationships is to meet in person. Soon or later you are going to have to meet in person and not hiding behind your emails or Social Media. Some people will only chat with you only online. They don't have any attention of meeting anybody in person. Part of networking is that you must communicate with others especially in person face to face. If you aren't the type to communicate with others face to face then networking will not work for you at all. One time there was a guy at a networking event who owns a travel business in Jersey City, NJ. We has spoken and exchange our contact information. He did invite me to connect with him on Facebook and Linkedin. I tried to call him several times and he always has an excuse for not meeting in person. Finally I told him that the purpose of networking is to do the follow up for the process of building relationship. He told me that I don't have time to follow up and building relationship. After that I told him then don't expect me to give you referrals for your travel business since you don't want to get to know each other. I also told him that I don't refer people to my network that I don't know or trust. After that I make sure that I hung up on him and tore up his business cards. If you want people to refer you or your business then you have to make an effort to follow up and to build solid relationships. People are going to do business with people that they know and trust. Build relationships with people you want to interact with and support. All else will follow from that. Just remember that supports go both ways and not one way.

There is a lot of people that will complain that networking don't work for them. They need to know that they are the one who isn't working their network. Are you working your network? They will not do their follow up with their prospect new connection. They are waiting for someone to call them. In networking if you are waiting for someone to call you then you will be waiting for a long time. You need to make the first move. New opportunity will not knock on your door. You must go after that opportunity. There's a woman I met at a networking event. Her name is Linda and she wasn't being friendly at all to the people who attended the event. I approached her and asked her **"How are You Doing Linda?"** She has given me a dirty look so I just walked away. I made sure that I will not be making a follow up call with her. What I am trying to say the reason why some people will not bother to get in contact with you because the way you presented yourself at the event. People will remember how you presented yourself at the event. People like to surround themselves with friendly and positive mindset individuals. Nobody doesn't want to be around with somebody that is always negative and miserable. The key to build that solid foundation of relationship is the follow up. When you are doing your follow up you need to do it right away so your presence can be still fresh in their mind. If you wait like six months later it will be hard to remember you unless you refresh their memory where they had met you at. Some individuals have a misunderstanding about networking concept. The development of building a strong network requires making those connections that will sustain more than an introduction. To develop a strong network you need the ingredients of those connections and the support that are requiring maintaining them. An initial meeting or contact with someone does not establish a connection unless you make an effort to do your follow-up of some kind. The follow-up must suggest a mutual interest in developing a meaningful supportive relationship.

Some people probably don't like to do follow up because they are not naturally more outgoing or outspoken. They are actually in fear of talking with people. You shouldn't let that discourage you from getting out there and meeting new people. Part of meeting new people while networking is to experience growth. Growth should be a part of everybody's agenda in their life. Without willing to have growth you will not have a successful networking experience or follow up. Networking is the product of focus and follow up to develop and nurture valuable relationships. That is the great recipe for establishing valuable relationships. One time a friend of mine Lynn has given my number to a person's name Willie who owns a Technology company. Anyhow he needed someone to do accounting for him. She only gave him my office number. He had to call the office number and didn't get an answer. He thought I had brushed him off. Lynn told me that she had given Willie my office number only because she didn't want to give him my cell number. I told her that If I have given you my cell number that's mean I want to use that number. Also give my cell number to people who are looking for my service. I had to give Willie a call and apologize to him for the misunderstanding. I told him that Lynn should have given him my cell number. He has forgiven me and told me that it was not my fault. He also told me that some people will never know anything about being professional. He finally told me what he was looking for his business. Since I couldn't help him personally, but I did refer him to somebody that I know who does have expertise of what he was looking for. He really appreciated it. Everybody is not going to do business with you, but they will give you referrals if you are willing to do your follow up and getting to know them by building solid relationships. Just remember that for you to have a successful experience is to make sure that you do your follow up and everything else will fall in place. Developing relationships is not just about contacts at all. Developing those relationships by doing your follow up is the key to having those accesses to different opportunities. Your value must be worth being willing to building relationships that are based on mutual needs and interests. You may meet your new contacts immediate, but a relationship can only be established and built over time by the process of the follow up. Credibility and trust are the stronger components to building relationships. Without those two components you will not be able to form any kind of relationships at all rather it is personal or professionals. The purpose to build up relationships begins with the first introduction and then requires the investment of your time and energy for the follow-up. The follow-up and continued contact is a prerequisite in developing relationships that will support your desire to be remembered. Making no efforts at all to follow-up or staying in touch with your potential connections then most likely your networking experiences will lead to dead ends. You had ended up wasting your time to give out your business cards because you didn't want to do your follow up. For you have a successful networking experience with potential connections you must have a mutual understanding from the beginning that networking is all about **"What I can do for you"** as you asking the same question **"What can you do for me."** That is what building your network is all about to make quality time and commitment to helping others. Networking is not only about meeting new people, but networking requires of you in showing concern and interest in others need that will help you to build that credibility and trust to establishing a great solid relationship.

I noticed when I attend networking events that you will always see representatives from MLM or network marketing companies. They are seen friendly at these events but most of them don't know how to network at these events. The first thing that they want to do is trying to recruit you into their network marketing business. They are always trying to recruit me to their MLM business regardless if they know I already have a successful business or involved with a network marketing company. Also when it is time to do the follow up most of them are not interesting in talking with you unless you join their business. I did a follow up with a person who was involved in an MLM company. When I finally gotten in contact with him, he didn't want to talk with me unless I was interested in joining his MLM Company. He did not want to build a solid relationship with me at all. That is one of the reasons why a lot of people are turned off by people who are involved in MLM companies. They don't know how to network with other professional. Some of them that I had witnessed for myself will bash somebody's business and will say their MLM business is better. I have news for you that everybody doesn't want to have no part in any MLM companies. You have to start building relationships with others by doing your follow up properly then once people start to get to know and trust you then maybe they will check out what you are doing with your MLM business.

I remembered one time, I called Roy that I met at a networking event and we had exchanged business cards. The next day I called him to do my follow up in the purpose to start building relationship with him. He wasn't having any of that, but all he wanted me to do is give him a presentation of what I do over the phone. I told him first of all I am here to get to know you and second I couldn't give you a presentation over the phone. When you are doing your follow up, you should not ask anyone to give you a presentation over the phone. Your purpose of the follow up is to get to know each other by building solid relationships. Also you should be able to set a date and time to meet up in person as well. Once you get to know each other for a while then you can start to talk about what you do with your business or career. You should only do your presentation in person and not over the phone or online.

How to Create More Meaningful Relationships:

- Be a Best Friend to others first (think about how you can give vs. receive)

- Identify who you want to build authentic relationships with (Best Connections happen when there are similar conscious levels and values)

- Create opportunities to know each other (take the first step- No need to wait!)

- Get to know them vs. Fringe Topics (Former builds true friendships; Latter builds superficial connections)

- Focus on positives, not negatives (see the beauty in each individuals)

- Share your life with them (Let them know)

- Build trust first (Nothing can develop w/o trust)

- Let them in during your down times (open up and let yourself be vulnerable)

- Be there for them when they need you (support, empathize, understand, don't impose)

- Focus on those who reciprocate your efforts (These are the gems and the keepers)

Milton Kelly

Chapter 8

The Networking Groups

"You Should Express Yourself into Success"

At every networking event there are usually run by an organization who is in charge of a networking group. There are so many networking groups to choose to be a part of. There are networking groups such as Business, Personal, Religions, Entertainment Industries and others. To be part of a networking group you need to become a member. You can't just go to a particular group event and expect people to support you if you aren't willing to become a member of that group. Remember that people will help others who they can trust and know. The organizers of most networking groups will tell their guests that they will only support their members of the group. If you aren't willing to be a team player then why should you expect them to help you?

Now before you join a networking group you should do your research about them. Find out what the group is all about and the purpose of the group. You should find out what the group has to offer to you for joining their networking group. Like two networking groups that I am part of GW Network and BDPA-NY Chapter of BDPA National. With GW Network by you become a member you paid a membership fee and the organizer will add your name in their business directory and also every time that they have an event you will pay a discount price. They also believe that everybody that belongs to this group should support each other with their products and services. By doing that you are bringing wealth in the community. With BDPA-NY you will become a member by paying an annual membership due. With that membership due they have so many benefits of being a member. They have monthly networking events, they have seminars dealing with business, educations and technology, they give scholarships to the youth for college, they have great programs with technology for youths, help you get a career in technology and have job fairs. They also have programs for entrepreneurs in Technology. This is an awesome networking group to be part of. They always keep you inform by emails, Social Media and quarterly magazines created by BDPA National. This group also has their national convention in the summer time in various cities. These are the types of networking groups that you should be part of.

There are some networking groups that all they want memberships and they won't offer anything. There was a Networking Group in New Jersey that had wanted me to pay almost $500.00 to join. I had thought it was kind of steep and also I didn't see any worth of my being part of that group. I have tried to do follow-up with several members but they didn't return my phone calls at all. If I don't see any value then I am not going to waste my time to join. I don't have anything against the group, but that wasn't the group I had the desire to be part of. There were another group that I have gone to their networking events, all you had to do was to join them by signing up at MeetUp.com to get an invite. You didn't have to pay a fee. So I decide to attend a couple of their events. They had over thousands of people attending the event. There were so many people that it was hard to talk to everybody at that event. There were some people that weren't even friendly at all. Then there were others that had spoken to me and I did my follow up with them. Personally I like small groups because it is easy for me to mingle with. Then it was a group that was consisted of in Harlem and they will have a networking event every month over breakfast. That was a great concept to network over breakfast. The only problem that I had with them were that they wanted you to become a member of the group by paying almost $500, but wouldn't offer you anything that they promised to offer you. Also the organizer didn't offer his support to me. Also he had felt since he already knew me that he didn't have to network with me. I don't care if I knew you for 20 years there is nothing wrong with us to network with, but we still need to mingle with others that we don't know. Since I wasn't willing to become a member I decided to stop attending that particular group events. If you aren't willing to become a member of that networking group regardless of the reasons, then you shouldn't attend their events. Some groups will not have you attend their events unless you have the desire to join their group.

It is great to be part of a networking group because you are part of a family. You are working together as a team. They will help you to be successful. They will empower, mentor, coach and encourage you in your purpose of networking. You will develop valuable relationships with your fellow members. You will have a better time of getting to know each other better because you both belongs to the same group. You most likely will follow up as well and build valuable relationships with each other's. If you aren't willing to be a team player then you don't need to be part of a networking group. Like I mentioned before there are several types of networking organizations to join in order to develop your professions through networking. It depends on your schedules you should start with two or three networking groups to start with. It doesn't matter with networking groups you want to be a member of.Just remember that you are not there to just sit there the whole time you at there. Also you are not there for the food that they are serving at the event. You are there to network means you are there to make sure that your network is working. Networking consists of work and not about the food or you are just sitting your butt on a chair. If you want to build your network for your business or career opportunity through word of mouth then you must work with the members of your networking group.

There are some networking groups that consider casual contact networks. Casual Contact Networks will allow many people from various overlapping professions. These groups don't have any restrictions on the number of people represented in any profession or industries. These kind of groups usually meets monthly and will often hold mixers so that will give the chance for people to mingle informally. Casual Contact networks might hold a special kind of meetings where there are presentations by guest speakers on important topics for business or discussions on issues such as community affairs, local business programs and legislations that will help the small business. The perfect examples of this kind of groups are the Chambers of Commerce and other groups that are similar active nationwide. These groups will offer individuals an opportunity to make valuable connections with many other entrepreneurs in that community. They will offer their support by helping to reach your goal of developing a word of mouth concept of business because they enable you to meet hundreds of their fellow business people.

Another kind of networking groups is Strong Contact Networks. Strong Contact Networks are networking groups that will meet weekly in the purpose of exchanging great referrals. These groups are purposely often restricted to membership to only one person per industries or profession. The main goals for that so there will be no competition in the same professions. Their events will have their meeting structured in a format include open networking in which everyone in the group will make a brief presentation about what they do. They will work together by giving each other business referral and support their fellow members by doing business with them as well. These kind of networking groups usually requires a commitment from their members. These groups will have a set agenda that you must abide by with the part of the meeting dedicated to actually give out referrals you have picked up from the members during the previous event. A great example of networking group is BNI. This particular group that I know of will not let no more than one person in a particular profession to join their group to prevent competitions at all. They might ask you to start a new chapter of that organization. They want to give their memberships a chance to do business without the competition.

Community Service Groups are a networking group that will give you the opportunity to give back to the community while you are networking with fellow members. This will be perfect for entrepreneurs for their business while making valuable connections and boosting your reputations as caring for the community that your business are located at. Your local community will really appreciate that you care about their community by getting involved. This networking group will be perfect for the opportunity to develop relationships in the community.

The Professional Associations are a networking group that has memberships associated with one specific type of industry such as Financial, Health, Legal, and others that have the primary focus of the group to exchange resources and ideas for that particular industry. Your purpose for the benefit of this kind of network is to get involved by becoming a member of that group will give you access to your potential target market or opportunity. You will know if this is a great group to join with their members retain their membership in the associations that will offer greater value that will benefit them.

There are different Women Organizations that you can be part of. This is the perfect networking group for women to be part of. There are a lot of great opportunities to network and work together. The members work well together by supporting and helping each others. Usually in this particular group that you will have women from all different industries. Some are professionals and others are entrepreneurs. They normally have events such as seminars, convention and networking events. They also do a lot for the community such as giving out scholarships to young women that are in High school or starting college. They have also mentored to these young ladies as well. These Women Organizations have some strong network connections. This group is very diverse. Again their concerns are with education and professional development. Their main purpose is to network. In this group they do offer professional support. The purpose of this group is for networking and not a club. The best thing about joining a group like this one that if you are in business then you don't have to worry about making cold calls because you had already made new connections by you making the effort to network.

There are so many networking groups that you can choose from to join. The best part by being part of a networking group that they can help you grow your network and connections. You are surrounded with other motivated entrepreneurs, professionals and business owners at a friendly atmosphere rather it is breakfast, lunch, dinner or a mixer after work. The purpose of that is to exchange ideas, contacts, strategies and experiences. This will be a great opportunity to connect with individuals who share your goals for success and will help you with your challenges. If you work your network right you may even meet a potential client or opportunity. In the community of the business world can be challenging but by getting involved with a networking group you can aggressive in your efforts to expand all networking opportunities to your fellow members and the community.

With all of these opportunities of networking there will be somebody will mention that they don't have time to network. You must make the sacrifice to make time for networking. There are only 24 hours a day, 7 days a week, 52 weeks a year and you have to spend some of that time sleeping, eating, playing, relaxing and experience that grows with yourself, your friends and your family. Time is the most precious resource so choose it wisely. You can always make time for networking if you really want to it. Once you waste that time you can't get it back. There is no quick fix about networking you must meet individuals in person in a planned and structured way. Whatever group that you decide to join please don't let chance to decide for yourself where you are going to spend your time and effort. The key in networking is to diversify your network and activities. Don't join the same kind of networking groups. You should join a mixture of different kind of networking groups. Remember the key of networking is being diversified. By you are joining only one kind of networking group won't serve all of your needs. You should select a mixture of networking organizations that will benefit you, your associates, partners or employees that you will target for.

Meetup.Com is another place to look for networking groups to join from different industries. Meetup.Com is a social media site for the purpose of networking. It is a great way to find the groups that you are interested in joining. You can also start your own group as well. Meetup.Com is the world largest network of local groups that will make it easy for anyone to organize a local group or find one of the thousands already meeting up face to face. There are more than 9,000 groups that will get together in local communities each day. Each one with the goal of improving themselves or their communities by networking. What I like about Meetup.Com is that their mission is to revitalize local community and help people around the world self-organize. This organization believes that people can change their personal world or the whole world by organizing themselves into groups like networking that are powerful enough to make a difference. I had used on this site as well to find new groups that I can be part of for the purpose to network. Everybody that likes to network should use this site for that purpose. The best part that it is free to join Meetup.Com.

Some people want to know if Networking groups really work, but the question should be asking **"Does networking groups really work for me?"** The answer to that question is they should work for you if you make an effort to work your network by making an effort to mingle with others and get involved with the group. For the networking groups work for you then you need to do the part by becoming a member and to participate in the group so that you will be noticed by the other members. If you are the type of a person that don't want to get involved or communicate with others then networking groups will not work for you at all. For those of us who been spending quality time networking that most likely we attend an event of networking group. I refer networking as hard networking that consists of hard work. Networking doesn't have room for being lazy at all. These networking groups want to stay active are still around. It must work for people that wanted it so bad otherwise the group won't survive at all. These individuals won't longer be part of that group. They have their reputation on the line. Most people join these groups by word of mouth the best way of marketing. If you want these individuals to give you referrals then you must do the same for others. Support goes both ways.

Just like in the Business world there are three types of people at networking events. There are **Go Getters, Slow Getters and No Getters.** The **Go Getters** are people that become successful at networking. They will end up with a lot of leads and a positive attitude. They will most likely to get the most referrals. Then you have the **Slow Getters** are people that will show up regularly but they aren't being successful in their quest rather if it is in their career or business. They do not give or receive many referrals at all. Finally you have the **No Getters** are people that will show up to a networking group for the first time. They will deliver their pitch but will complain that nobody wants to talk with them or do business with them. At the conclusion they will decide not to attend that group event ever again. Some will even bash the group and tried to discourage others from not attending.

If you want to be successful with these networking groups you must be a **Go Getters** and not a **Slow Getters** or a **No Getters.** You must sell the network and not the Networker. When you are going to an event giving by networking groups your purpose should not be about selling your services to each other at all. Your purpose is to network and start the process of developing long term relationships. Once you establish that long term relationship then maybe you will be able to do business with each other's. The purpose of developing long term relationships for familiarity and trust. You ask yourself the following questions when you are at a networking group event **"How valuable are you to the other members in the group?" "Can They Trust You With Their Referrals?" "Are You Willing to share your resources such as referring your friends, family members, connections to your fellow members?"** These are the question that you need to think about. If you aren't willing to share your resources then you don't need to be part of a networking group. When I was working with Primerica, I used to give individuals referral of my connections. But when I asked them for referrals then they will make excuses that either it's a conflict or they will not return my calls. When you only want people to do things to benefit you but aren't willing to give back to others then you are being selfish. Again support goes both ways. If you aren't receiving referrals then asked yourself, **"How many you willing to give out to others are?"** If you aren't going to give out referrals then don't expect to receive any at all. There is an old sayings that we will say in Church each week if you are a blessing to someone then somebody will be a blessing to you. When blessings go up then the blessings will come down. You better believe that. When you help somebody like their business not only they will appreciate it, but they will always remember what you has done for them. When you need some help they will have no problem of helping you.

The important question that we should be asking ourselves when we about to join a networking group **"Is I am a type of a person that like to make friends?"** or **"If I am likeable?"** If you can't answer those two questions then you are going to have a problem with these groups. If you make a wrong impressions to others in the group then nobody isn't going refer anything to you. When you are at the networking groups' event you have to be on your best behavior and be friendly to others. Nobody doesn't want to be around with anyone that is miserable. They aren't going to let you mess up their reputations at all. You have to be a good fit with others in the group. Also the group has to be a great fit for you as well since you are going to be paying your membership fee to join the group. If you know in your heart that the group is not a great fit for you then don't waste your time or money in that particular group and find another group to be a member of. Also you should find a networking group that met at the time that are best for you to work around your busy schedule. If you know that the meeting is early in the morning like 7:30 AM and you know that you aren't a morning person then you shouldn't attend their event. You should pick a networking group that has an event in the afternoon or in the evening that way you don't waste your time or theirs.

If there isn't a networking group that meets your needs then you can always start your own networking group. This is the best way for you to create a strong network by is to create your own network. Plant your presence and others will follow you. You just need to pick a perfect time and place that will work for you. You can start a group of Social Media like Facebook, Linkedin, Google Plus and Meetup.Com. I had created a networking group on Facebook recently called **"Create Your Own Opportunity Network Group."** The purpose of me creating my group on Facebook is to network with others. Also share information and resources with others as well. I do interact with the members regularly to try to keep the group active. I even encourage the members to share what they are feeling or promote in what they do. I want everybody to get to know each other. That's how a relationship is blossom by spending quality time to get to know each other. Sometimes when you start your own networking group you can always form a partnership with companies or other networking groups. The purpose of partnership is to create opportunity for building a stronger network. Now there was one networking group that I was part of in Jersey City, NJ. I don't want to mention the group name, but I found this group on Meetup.Com. I had to admit it was a great group to be part of because of the members.

Everybody in the group was very friendly. We use to meet for lunch once a month for our networking event at a diner on Route 440. The group wasn't big because the organizer at the time didn't want the group to be big. He told me that he like small group because that way you can mingle better. Not only that it was a lunch event but there was always a guest speaker. The only problem that I had with the group was that the members don't believe to follow up. Also when I invite them to others networking events that I will attend, then they never want to go. One day the organizer of that networking group decide to resign because his schedule was very busy. So this new guy named Ron took over the group, but he never stays in contact with us. He didn't even work with the group. About six months later the group was broken up. The factor was that nobody didn't want to be part of it. I seen a lot of networking groups are up running one day then the next day the group doesn't exist anymore. If you want to keep your networking group active you have to invite new members to join. Stay in touch with your members regularly just to show that you care about them. Offer your members something in value so they will stay in your group and refer others to the group. Some people will just start a networking group just to make money so they can pay off their mortgage. They don't have anything to offer to their members. You need to stay away from those kinds of groups. If I don't see any value in the group then I will not be joining at all especially if the membership fee is over $300.00.

When you start your own network you can target professionals who can refer opportunities your business or your professional career. Also you will do the same as well. You can send them invitations to join your network. As they become your members they are adding value to your groups by helping your network to grow even stronger. Most likely they are going to invite their network to your networking groups as well. You will become the center of influence with your network. Everybody in your network wants to help you to succeed. That's what networking all about to help others to reach their goals by working together in harmony.

My favorite quote from Zig Ziglar had mentioned **"You can get whatever you want if you can just help enough other people get what they want."** This is an excellent life learned lesson to live by being an example of helping others.

The purpose for you to start your own networking group is to establish connections with other professionals to expand your network such gathering new connections and opportunities. This is very important for your goals of networking to be successful. You definitely want to develop relationships in persons by face to face connections with the local business community to establish a support network and successfully obtaining new opportunities. Your support network of like-minded professionals and entrepreneurs can always offer you some great advice and expertise when you need it the most. The best part of starting your own networking group is that there are no limited opportunities for networking if it is done correctly. Starting a new networking group of your own is not going to be easy. There are going to be a lot of hard work than showing up to another group event. The benefit of starting your own networking group is to make sure that you are establishing a custom tailored group. That will really be worth of the effort of your goals to expand your network. You should start small by having a handpicked membership by finding the right people with mutual things in common. You can start with one or two professionals that you have a great chemistry with and where you might want to target the same market but within different industries. You really don't want to compete with each other's. By you both are working with different industries then in time you both can bring others in the group and grow it successfully.

You must have a vision or a plan when you are going to start your own networking group. How do you want your networking group to look like? What is the mission of the group? What is the purpose of creating this group? What do you expect from the memberships? Are you looking to give back to the community? What kind of events that you will like to plan? Who will you put in charge of the group? Those are some of the questions that you want to ask yourself when you are starting a group. I know somebody that has a networking group in the metropolitan area of New York City and he started that group a few years ago. The person wanted the group to be big without starting small or having a plan. He already wanted to start chapters in different states, but he didn't have his main group solid yet. We all tried to tell him to work with this main group first and once you had successfully maintain the group then you start your second chapter. It is just like running a franchise like McDonalds. When you are starting to operate your McDonalds Franchise you will open your first franchise. You will not open 100 franchise at the same time. You will work with your first franchise to make sure that it will run successfully. Once you know that your McDonalds franchise is successful then you will open your second one and more by following the simple rules of running a business correctly. I would recommend you to read Leesa Barnes Article **"5 Ways to Start a Networking Group That Sizzles and Not Fizzles."** She mentioned in her article that you have an understanding of why you're creating your networking group by crafting a winning purpose and strategies for the upcoming year. There is a saying in the Business World that without a plan or goals that you will fail. If you are looking for a casual but a small group like a monthly gathering then the organization will not be a concern at all. You need to be willing to have an interest in attracting new members by expanding your network. That is what you call growth. In life we all need to have growth in our daily lives and networking can surely do that for us. You also have to be a great leader to have a successful networking group. You must take on a leadership role so you can establish structure in your group like creating a mission statement and the rules of the groups in which I called it the bylaws.

Just like to have a successful business, for you to have a successful networking group and networking experiences you must have that momentum. The purpose of your networking group that you have started is to make it a success. The reason why a lot of networking groups doesn't last because they don't have the momentum. You need to stick with your group that you had started. It can be a lot of work to maintain the networking group bit it will all be worthy of you to maintain some momentum. It's easy to start a group but it is hard to keep it running without momentum. You need to give your members for reasons for them to keep coming back and refer people to your group. I belonged to a networking group for a short time in 2010 and every month they will have the same kind of event and never will offer something different so at the end people had lost interest to come back. After a while the group dissolved because they have lost their momentum. If they have kept the group interesting. Also gotten feedback from the members then that group will still exist today. Again you have to show value for them to keep their membership in your group.

Another way that you can benefit from having a successful networking group is to get online for networking. Start a website for your networking group. Make sure that you start a Facebook Page for your networking group. Even I will use Linkedin and other Social Media sites to promote my networking group. Even in the technology world you can make that work in your favor. The best site to promote face to face networking opportunities is Meetup.com. Meetup.com is a website that will help users to schedule, organize and promote networking events in person. You will get a chance to find individuals that are like minded networkers in your surrounding area. You can also set up RSVPS and payment for that event. Finally you can send reminders about your networking events so they won't forget. EventBrite.com is another website that will provide online tools to manage and promote your networking events. EventBrite.com will also contact the attendees, set up registration into your own websites and to collect payments for the event. A lot of people are starting to use EventBrite.Com to their events that they are having. You will get a list of people who you are expecting to attend your event. EventBrite.com will charge a commission fee for your events depending on the cost of your event. Also you can post your events that are free and listed at no cost at EventBrite.com.

Just like to have a successful business, to have a successful networking group and networking experiences you must have that momentum. The purpose of your networking group that you have started is to make it a success. A lot of networking groups doesn't last because they don't have the momentum. You need to stick with your group that you had started. It can be a lot of work to maintain the networking group bit it will all be worthy of you to maintain some momentum. It's easy to start a group but it is hard to keep it running without momentum. You need to give your members for reasons for them to keep coming back and refer people to your group. After a while the group had dissolved because they have lost their momentum. If they have kept the group interesting and got feedback from their members then that group will still exist today. Again you have to show value for them to keep their membership in your group. .

Every time that you are having events please invite someone from the community to be a guest speaker. They can share their expertise from being a web guru, government official, a representative from the Small Business Associations, Community Leaders and successful Business Owners. You should be up to date on current events and you should invite speakers to address those issues concerning the entire community at your event. That will show your potential members that you really care about the community. Speaking of the community you should definitely make an effort to give back to the community. Offer scholarships to the individuals in your local community that want to further their education. You should organize an annual opportunity in service by helping out in your local community like doing a park cleanup, volunteer at a local Food Pantry or organize a cloth drive for the needy. People will get involved with groups that are doing charity works for the community. My final thought on having an event with your networking group.

Sometimes you are going need to change the location of your events. You need to mix your events with of a variety. It could be a lunch meeting one month, breakfast meeting the next month. Also once in a while maybe have an after hour work mixer at a restaurant that have an awesome bar that people had always wanted to check out but didn't get a chance to go. Also by having your events at that particular restaurant you will definitely can expand your network including adding the restaurant owner. She/he can add value to your group because they can share their connections with you and the members of the group. You can also have your networking events in an art gallery looking at some wonderful pictures. That will be another way to grow your network. The Arts community is very big when coming to network. By you have different kinds of events then you will be able to attract new members to join and they will stick around because they will see the value. You will also give great exposures for you and your networking group.

In Summary of The Real

Purpose of Networking

"It isn't just what you know, and it isn't just who you know. It's actually who you know, who knows you, and what you do for a living." Bob Blurg

Now you should know how important for you to know what your real purpose of networking all is about. You should realize by now that networking is essential to our business and career opportunities. When we use the tools of effective networking we are experiencing the wisdom in a nutshell of new opportunities that will come our way. Networking will help you discover hidden opportunities and separate you from the competition. We can start networking with somebody that we already know that can lead us to their connections that we need to get in contact with. You now know how you can overcome your shyness and fear of rejection.

As you finished reading this book you should learn about how to build a partnership with networking for new opportunities. Now that you are networking you will be able to reach your potential target of individuals either directly or indirectly. You should learn that you can network in different ways beyond going to networking events. You had learned that the importance of building your network is a process that still ongoing. You should always increase your range of contacts daily. You also had learned that your purpose of networking is about support. Support goes both ways and not one way. Networking is all about building relationship by getting to know each other. As you are getting to know each other by making an introduction and what can you offer to each other by sharing resources and contacts. We know how important partnership is when we are networking. You should be talking with everyone that you know that may have opportunities. Offer what partnership that you can offer and the purpose of that partnership. Picking the best contact that will help you in partnerships in expanding your network. We know that communications are the keys to successful networking experiences. By connecting with the right people that know a lot of contacts can be a blessing to you and your personal network.

We need to learn that from us growing or expanding our network we need to be where everybody will be at. You now know that in networking that you must be able to hold a conversation with others.

Again Communication is the key to networking. Just exchanging business cards is not considered by networking at all. You must get that key information about your potential connection. We know that by networking we don't have to worry about making cold calls because we already made the effort to get to know them. Follow up is the most part of networking to be successful because without it you will not have a successful networking experience at all. Follow up is all about getting to know each other in the process of building relationships. You know that you should always be positive, cheerful, confident and friendly when you are networking. You will not wait for someone to follow up with you instead you will take charge by making the first attempt to follow up with that person. When you are at an event you will not wait for someone to talk with you. You will be the one to start the conversation with that person. You will know how to build solid relationship with others. You will actually know what common interests that you and your potential connections have. You will know when to speak and when not to speak because you are taking the time to listen to the other person. That is part of communication. Good relationship just doesn't happen overnight but it is a process. In this world people will not do business or offer opportunities to people who they don't know or trust.

In this book we now know that the importance of being part of a networking group and the benefits of being part of one. We know what to expect by becoming a member of a networking group. You will know what to look for when looking to be part of a networking group. There are several different kinds of networking group to choose from. You will know if you are a great fit or not to be part of that particular group. You should know that if you want the benefit of the group then you need to be part of that group. You also learn about how to start your own networking group to expand your network. You learn about how to be part of a local community that you have your networking events at for your group. By being part of a group you are in harmony with your fellow members and the organizer of the group.

We now know the importance of doing our follow up. Networking doesn't officially start until we start with our follow up. The follow up is the key in having a successful networking experience. Without the follow up you will not do well in your networking experience. The Follow up is the process of building relationships. Building relationships is the key for networking. Building a solid relationships are based on trust and honesty. Building solid relationships are more about giving support to each other. It's about getting to know each other. People will not recommend me you unless they know you pretty well. They want to recommend people that they know and can trust. They do not want their reputations to be ruined at all. You should now know that you don't wait for someone that you had met at a networking function to get in contact with you but you have to take the first step. You now know that you can do your follow up in a different way of channels that you can choose from.

We also know that our behavior should be professional at all time. Networking is a professional tool to connect with others. We should always be on our best behavior at all time. Our appearance should always be our best as well. Just like if we are going on a job interview or a business meeting that we should dress in our best either in business attire or casual business attire. Remember that when we are networking that we are representing a brand. We are marketing ourselves so we should be able to make an everlasting impression. Now that you know the different ways on how you can network successfully you are should be a pro about networking. Practice makes perfect. Just like in music, acting, sports and others that require perfection you must practice first to master the task. Even when you are making mistakes you will learn from them.

Acknowledgments

I am thankful to Jesus Christ for saving me and allowing me to accept Him as my personal savior. I am thanking Him for blessing me with a new door open as the previous door was closed. I am grateful that I am blessed and know that I know Him for myself.

I am thankful to Jesus Christ for saving me and allowing me to accept Him as my personal savior. I am thanking Him for blessing me with a new door open as the previous door was closed. I am grateful that I am blessed and know that I know Him for myself.

Thanks for the following Churches that had supported me throughout the years. Christ Fellowship Baptist Church of Brooklyn, NY (Reverend Dr. David L. Kelley II), Union Baptist Church of White Plains, NY (Reverend Dr. Verlin Williams), First Baptist Church of Crown Heights Brooklyn, NY (Reverend Clarence Normans Sr.), Mount Lebanon Baptist Church, Brooklyn, NY (Reverend Shaun Lee), Springfield Baptist Church of Washington D.C.

I want to thank my mother Annie Jewell Kelly, my sisters Yvette and Delores Kelly for your support. Thanks to Trey Williams of Cincinnati, Ohio for always being there for me especially during my rough time. You are a great friend and I Love you for being in my life. Paul A. Chung of Jersey City, NJ for being a great friend to me for the last two decades.

Special Thanks to Carl June of CarlLu Productions of Staten Island, NY for being a great friend throughout the years and especially during my difficult times. You had really been a great friend to me. Thanks for always having my back and always encouraging me to me in writing this book. I wish you all the success with your movies and business in the film industry. You are a great mentor to me. I will never forget what you had done for me.

Special Thanks to Elois Thames, CEO of Rare Diamond Publication,

Flint, Michigan for allowing me to interview on her blog to promote my book **"Walking In God's Path Toward Your Destination Volume 1" To Change Your Mindset**. You had really given me the opportunity for promoting my book.

Special thanks also go out to Desiree Spivey, Image Consulting of "A New You Image Consulting" from New York City, NY for being a great friend to me. You had always been very professional and kind to me. I had really enjoyed our conversation and giving me some great advice about my future in writing my book. Thanks for teaching me on how to network with others. Cathy Payne **(The Story Princess)** of Bronx, NY and Los Angeles, CA. I want to personally thank you for being there for me during my difficult time. You really supported me in my writing. You gave many great advice about on how creating my own opportunities.

I want to give a special shout out to my favorite Networking Group BDPA-New York of accepting me in their group. It's a pleasure of being a part of this wonderful group of professionals and business owners. It's always great to network with all of you at BDPA.

I want to thank Georgia Woodbine of GW Network for encouraging me to write my book even I didn't believe I couldn't write one. I want to thank my Pastor Reverend Dr. David L. Jefferson Sr. Pastor and teacher of Metropolitan Baptist Church of Newark, NJ for teaching and preaching empowering sermon to change my life. You always teach us that, **"When one door is close that God will open another door in my life."** I now know that just because I did lose my job, it doesn't mean my life isn't over. You really taught me about walking in victory because I am a Child of God and surround myself in the Word of God. God Bless you!

I want to thank Glen & Xiomara LI and the Dragon Team of Primerica Financial Services of Edison, New Jersey for giving me a chance in working with you all and welcoming me to your group. I had learned a lot from this great company. You had taught me on how to be a great leader and I can work for myself and be successful in life. You are the reason that I am writing my books that are self-published.

I want to give special thanks to Bridge Street Development Corporation of Brooklyn, NY for giving me the opportunity of teaching about the importance of having Life Insurance at your First Home Buyers Seminar. I also want to thank Robert Glassman of Sharon, MA being a great friend and showing his kindness toward me.

Special Blessings To The Following: Eula Young the owner at Giriot's Roll Film Production of Harlem, NY, Pastry Chef Danielle Moore the owner and operator at Annie Mae's Bakery of Brooklyn, NY, Darryl Cherry of Somerset, NJ, Annette Bland-McCoy of New York City, NY, Dartel McRae of New York City, NY, Barbara Smith and Dan Gasby of B.Smith Restaurant of New York City, NY, Tonya Parrott –Carlisle of New York City, NY, Phyllis Cameron of Sanford, NC, April Suddreth of New York City, NY, Cynthia Cameron- Stewart of Sanford, NC, The Celestial Community Choir of Brooklyn, NY, The North New Jersey Chapter of GMWA, Lisa D. Nelson and the Mass Choir of Union Baptist Church of White Plains, NY, The Ambassadors of Christ Choir of Christ Fellowship Baptist Church of Brooklyn, NY, Derek Hawkins of Maplewood, NJ, Betty Long Owner of Gospel Den from Brooklyn, NY, DeDe Kridge of Los Angeles, CA, Donna Jarrett and It Takes A Village Organization of Brooklyn, NY, Joe Long Owner of Birdells Records of Brooklyn, NY, Roger and Terry Harris of New York City, NY, Melba Thomas and Melbas Restaurant of Harlem, NY and Pastor David L. Kelley II and his lovely wife First Lady Kim Kelley of Christ Fellowship Baptist Church of Brooklyn, NY. A special thank you to the Hickson Family of Brooklyn, NY: Joann Hickson, Jonathan Hickson, Jennifer Hickson and her son Jordan Simon for showing their kindness to me.

ABOUT THE AUTHOR

Milton Kelly is an Author of two books "Walking In God's Path Toward Your Destination Volume 1" To Change Your Mindset and "Walking In God's Path Toward Your Destination Volume 2" Building A Personal Relationship With Him. Both books are Inspirational books that will help individuals to overcome their issues and changing their attitude about life. The purpose of these two books helps individuals to have a better spiritual walk with God. Milton Kelly was born and raised in Brooklyn, NY in the section of Bedford Stuyvesant. He currently resides in Jersey City, NJ. Milton had worked for Morgan Stanley Dean Witter for the past 18 ½ years until late 2007. Then he took the opportunity to work with Primerica Financial Services for 3 ½ years until early this year as an Independent Representative. He is a member of the BDPA-NY and the Gospel Music Workshop of America National Convention. Milton believes in networking to build solid relationships. He is an expert on how to create a great relationship by networking. He is currently the creator of Create Your Own Opportunity Network Group. Milton is a freelance writer with the Yahoo Contributors Network.

You can check out Milton Kelly's First Two Books "Walking In God's Path Toward Your Destination Volume 1" To Change Your Mindset and "Walking In God's Path Toward Your Destination Volume 2" Building A Personal Relationship With Him. Both books are available for purchase online at Amazon. Both books are also available in the format of Kindle Download. Here is the link: http://www.amazon.com/author/miltonkelly92

Here is Milton's Blog Link: http://miltonkelly.wordpress.com/

Twitter: https://twitter.com/Kellym209

Milton's Facebook Fan Page:
https://www.facebook.com/AuthorMiltonKelly92